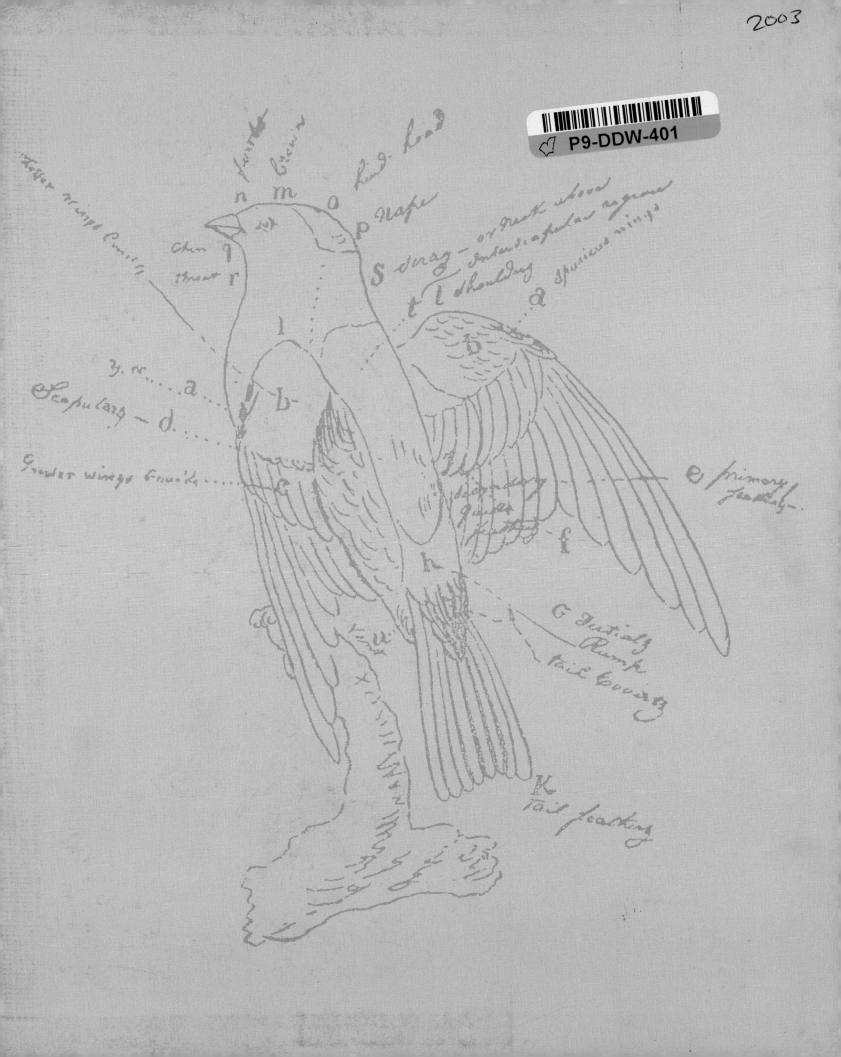

2003

Into the Woods

For Ian Madden Roberts (and Jean and Chris)—R. B.

In memory of Joel Strever: fellow artist, friend, and mentor—W. M.

AUTHOR'S NOTE

John James Audubon was a famous early American woodsman and artist. Despite his father's objections, Audubon had to follow his own special destiny. This story consists of an imaginary letter in which Audubon explains to his father why he has chosen the unique life he leads. In addition, quotations in script, taken from Audubon's journals, further emphasize the profound world view of this remarkable man.

Atheneum Books for Young Readers
An imprint of Simon & Schuster Children's Publishing Division
1230 Avenue of the Americas
New York, New York 10020

The following images by John James Audubon are courtesy of the New York Historical Society:
Title page and page 16: Violet-green swallow (1863.17.385), page 8: Northern cardinal (1863.17.159),
page 12: Great cormorant (1863.17.266), page 20: Broadwinged hawk (1863.17.091),
page 24: Mallard Gadwell hybrid duck (1863.17.338), page 28: Mourning dove (1863.17.017),
and page 32: Black-throated green warbler (1863.17.399)

Book design by Wendell Minor
Art direction by Ann Bobco
The text of this book is set in 16-point Centaur and 24-point Shelley Allegro.
The display type is set in Sisman.
The illustrations are rendered in watercolor.

Manufactured in China

2 4 6 8 10 9 7 5 3
Library of Congress Cataloging-in-Publication Data
Burleigh, Robert.
Into the woods : John James Audubon lives his dream / Robert Burleigh ; illustrated by Wendell Minor.—1st ed.
p.   cm.
ISBN 0-689-83040-8
1. Audubon, John James, 1785–1851—Juvenile literature. 2. Naturalists—United States—Biography—Juvenile literature.
3. Artists—United States—Biography—Juvenile literature. [1. Audubon, John James, 1785–1851.
2. Naturalists. 3. Artists. 4. Diaries.] I. Minor, Wendell, ill. II. Title.
QL31.A9 B87 2002
598(.092—dc21
[B]   2001022954

ROBERT BURLEIGH

Into the Woods

John James Audubon Lives His Dream

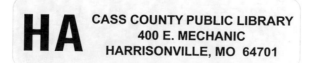

PAINTINGS BY WENDELL MINOR

ATHENEUM BOOKS FOR YOUNG READERS
NEW YORK LONDON TORONTO SYDNEY SINGAPORE

"Be a store owner," his father said.
But John went to the woods instead.

"Mind your business, save every cent."
But into the woods John Audubon went. . . .

The forest is the only place in which
I truly live. . . . Without any
money, my talents are my
support and my enthusiasm is my guide in
my difficulties.

My only ambition is (said he)
To leave a record of all I see,

Who can imagine my dear country's

dark woods, its great forests, its

vast Atlantic bays, its thousands of

streams, lakes, and magnificent rivers?

I wish that I could draw it all!

To mark the hummingbird's zigzag flight,
To glean the owl by firelight,

To climb the high cliff's rocky sides,
And find the ledge where the cormorant hides,

I lay flat on the edge of a cliff, a hundred feet above the wild waters. By crawling along carefully, I came within a few yards of the spot where the parent bird was taking care of her young.

To peek out through the river grass,
And see the great blue heron pass,

To wake up with the sun and row
To the island retreat where the seabirds go.

Wading knee-deep through mud and water,
I was soon on the small island where the bird was
comfortably seated on her nest. Softly and on
all fours I crept to the spot. Lovely creature!
How innocent! There she sits on her eggs, her
eyes half-closed, as if she dreamed of future scenes.

To listen close and hear the hum
Where in the twilight swallows come,

Or watch the egrets by the shore
Stand silently—all this and more.

They stood like statues of pure

white stone, forming a fine contrast

to the deep blue sky.

O Father, dear Father, to me it seems
No one can fail who holds to his dreams.

Ever since I was a boy I have had a

great desire to see and understand

the world of animals and birds.

This morning on my morning walk
I spied inside its nest a hawk.

I brought it down and home with me,
Wrapped in a cloth, so tenderly.

It lay quietly in the handkerchief.
I carried it home and went to my
room, where I began to draw it
right away.

See—how on my desk it stood
(Its talons clutched a stick of wood).

My eye on its, its eye on mine.
Divided by the thinnest line.

No sound except my scratching pen,
My measuring tools, my chalk, and when

My brush had got each color right,
From dark tail band to beak's blue white,

I let it go and watched it fly,
A tiny speck against the sky.

I put the hawk on a stick nailed to my table. It didn't move.
Its eye stared into mine. I picked up my pencil and drew,
without the creature ever moving once. When the drawing was
finished, I raised the window and let the bird go free. It sailed
off until it was out of my sight, without uttering a single cry.

O Father, Father, my dream is this:
To paint each creature as it is!

Some inward feeling tells me when
my work is good. No one, I think,
draws and paints the way I do. I
finish a picture at one sitting—
sometimes I sit for fourteen hours—
until I think it is right and true.

Last April on the hill above,
Father, I held a dying dove.

I saw its rich metallic hues,
I saw its reds and greenish blues.

I saw its soft and timid gaze.
I saw its golden feathers blaze.

How I gazed at its colorful feathers!
How I looked into its large and
timid eye, as this most beautiful of
woodland cooers was gasping its
last breath!

And as I watched it die I knew
The world I love is passing too.

And I must paint it all because
We need this memory of what was—

When I see settlers cutting down the forest trees to
make way for towns and farms, I pause and wonder.
These changes have all taken place in the short period
of twenty years. Although I know it is true, I can
scarcely believe it is real.

The long-necked loon with its strange wail,
The flycatcher with its thin, forked tail,

The spoonbill with its wide webbed feet,
The prairie chick, the parakeet,

From pigeon flocks that block the sun
To every kind of bird, each one.

The air was thick with pigeons.
They darted forward in great waves.
When they rose up high in the air,
they wheeled and twisted like the
coils of a gigantic serpent.

But listen, now, from every tree
I hear them calling out to me:

The crow's *ka-kow*, the lark's *ti-ti,*
The warbler and the chickadee.

*These cries are unlike the sounds of any musical
instrument. They resemble the syllables "kewrr,"
"kewrr," "kewrooh." And strange as these
bird cries are, they have always sounded
delightful in my ear.*

Fear not, Father, I'm true to you.
I have my whole life's work to do:

To go into these woods again,
To see, to feel, to learn, and then,

To draw all that I look upon. . . .
Your loving son,
John Audubon

I have seen this, and I am content.

*J*ohn James Audubon is one of America's most famous painters and naturalists. He came to America as a young man from France in 1803. Already a talented artist, he became fascinated with America's wilderness and its wildlife, especially birds. After failing at several attempts to be a businessman (because he preferred to walk about and study and draw in the woods), he devoted the rest of his life to his art. His ambition was to paint every bird species in North America.

His pictures are remarkable for their accuracy, their vivid color, and their dramatic presentations. Although Audubon hunted and often killed the birds he drew, he had a keen appreciation for wildlife and the environment. When he died in 1851, he was one of the most beloved artists in the United States. Today, he is seen as an early champion of preserving America's rich inheritance of plant and animal life.

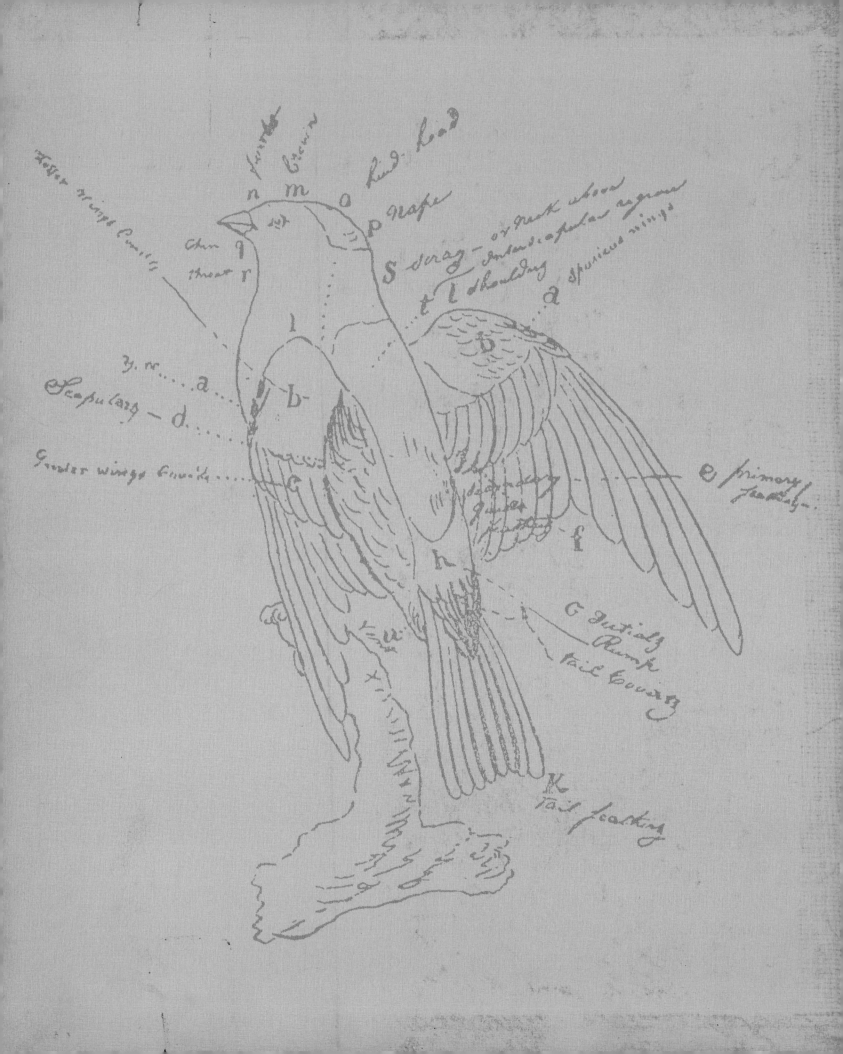